LILAC SKIES

By: Sarah Reese

Dedicated to:

My first love, for loving me more than I could myself.

Table of Contents:

Table of Contents Continue:

for·get

fərˈget/

verb

fail to remember.

fail to remember, fail to recall, fail to think

inadvertently neglect to attend to, do, or mention something.

put out of one's mind; cease to think of or consider.

verb: forget; 3rd person present: forgets; past tense: forgot; gerund or present participle: forgetting; past participle: forgotten

love

ləv/Submit

noun

1.

an intense feeling of deep affection.

”babies fill parents with intense feelings of love”

synonyms: deep affection, fondness, tenderness, warmth, intimacy, attachment, endearment; More

heart·break

ˈhärtˌbrāk/Submit

noun

noun: heartbreak; plural noun: heartbreaks

overwhelming distress.

"an unforgettable tale of joy and heartbreak"

Green Tea

I'll sip my green tea, steaming,
Every sip burning my lips,
But the pain doesn't reach my soul.
For that was lost long ago, in boxes stacked high in the attic.
I could spend a day trying to find it, and I'm sure it would appear,
In the box labeled "past lovers", who no longer are here.
I could spend a day sewing it back together, until it felt just right,
But the fabric would still be loose and the warmth it once brought is no longer here,
For that is in the letter, titled "my dear".
I could spend a day injecting it into me and feel the high your presence once brought
But you lost that privilege the day you walked out on me.
I could spend a day tracking you down just so I could find my happiness that you hold hostage
But moving is so hard since you left.
I could spend a day begging you to let my poisoned heart go
But you would laugh and send me on my way
For I was nothing more than the bug you killed on our first date.
I could spend a day listening to our song hoping to find any clues of why you left me stranded
With nothing but a box of tea and dead roses.
I could spend a day trying to take off the ring you gave me the night I told you "I love you"

But it's still holding on to any remaining hope that you might
turn around and remember all those things you said long ago.
I could spend a day saying nothing at all but just sitting and
remembering that night at the bar.
I could spend a day crying until my room became the ocean
which upon I would sail away,
But I'm too scared the hurricane
Named after you would crush my tiny ship named hope
And I would be stranded on the island of lonely & depression.
I could do all these things until a year flew by, and the hope
that you would remember would still be standing strong.
I could beg, dig and cry and all the things I could do to win
back you
But you wouldn't give me a glance for I'm just the girl who
was stuck in pretend.
I'm just the girl, that you once loved, but you can't even
remember all the years we spent,
But here I am, drinking my tea, and every word you said is
pressed into me as if I am a newspaper, for the lost and lonely.
I sip my green tea, burning my lips.
Reminding me of you and your cruel intent.

Why I hate Columbia road:

My hands shake on the steering wheel. A clear sign that I am terrified.

I'm terrified.

I'm terrified I'm going to wake up one day and realize I'm no longer yours. I'm so scared that one day I won't be able to slip my hand into yours, or harass you for a kiss.

I'm scared the rain won't make me smile anymore but instead bring tears to my eyes because it's not raining where you are.

I'm scared I won't be able to look at you while you drive, concentration written on your face like a newspaper, except when changing the song.

I'm scared that when I say I love you, one day you won't say it back.

Read at 2:45 am.

I'm scared that one day you won't respond to my text because you are ignoring me, not because you hate texting.

I'm scared that one day I won't get the chance to write you a love letter.

I'm grasping onto you and you are slipping out of my hands like water split out of a glass that fell from a table.

You ask me why I hate Columbia road, and I use to laugh and say I don't but I hate that road.

A road full of trees, their branches reaching into me ripping out every emotion in me and leaving it on the

concrete to be run over by everyone else. Buckle up, it's bumpy.
Can you please swerve?
My eyes are screaming, can you not hear? Please don't go.
I'm scared.
I'm terrified.
I'm scared that you don't care, please let me know because it's like putting me in a shredder and getting stuck: I'm bleeding.
Tape me together again.
Scrape me off the pavement and tell me you love me.
I hate Columbia road.
Sjr
8/8/16

Cancer

He was embedded in the plastic of a moldy lawn chair;
Clinging on to his Newport and his facade of popularity.
Nobody missed him, nobody spoke his name, but you couldn't miss the manifest feeling of him that hung in the halls by rusty nails.
He is the feeling of a cough, but when you move your chest to remove him, nothing but dry air comes out and the increasingly haunting feeling of being choked from the inside out over whelms you.
He no longer stood in the back hallway, smoke circling around him as he stood observing, but every time you pass it you get a whiff of polo cologne and tobacco; The invisible memorial of him.
They said they found him, clinging to his heart, on the tiles of his upstairs bathroom. His parents say it was suicide, i know deep down inside he died from the hypothermia of isolation.
They called him crazy, they called him insane but that doesn't stop the fake tears that split from their faces as if they were empty glasses with a milk stain.
Although people can't seem to remember, they can't seem to forget, that the boy in the back of the chemistry class was now nothing more than the ashes of his unlit cigarette.
sjr // 12-18-15

Untitled

You left a box of new ports in my car, along with your lucky lighter. I keep it in the glove box because I secretly hope one day, you'll ride once again in the passenger seat of this old 2009 Honda civic. Holding my hand and thumping your other hand to the beat of a journey song. Maybe one day we can roll up the windows once again and hot box while jamming to High and Dry by radio head, leaving burnt cannabis on my cloth seat. And after the blunt ran out you would light up your new ports and laugh about the face I made when I smelt it.

You left your favorite CD in my CD player, full of all the songs you listened to when you felt down. And sometimes when I'm going 70 on a country road, I roll down my windows and turn the volume all the way up and scream along to the lyrics. I keep it in the CD player because I hope one day you'll call me up for a ride, and I can accidently turn it on and maybe the words can seep into you and remind you of me, us and everything we use to be.

You left your old sunglasses in the holder and sometimes when I can't see I'll put yours on instead of mine, because you always said I looked beautiful when I did it with you, and maybe one day I'll pull up next to you and you'll see me, and you'll do a double take and realize I'm wearing your old pair of black ray bands, the pair you've been looking for. Everything you once said in the front seat of my car will pour back into you all because of the way the sun hits my hair and your sunglasses lay on my nose.

What is music?

Your favorite song played on the radio yesterday while I was speeding down William few and for the first time since you left I didn't change the station, no I listened and let the words soak into me. I believe through that song I finally understand why you did what you did. The words mumbling answers to questions I've been waiting to hear. In that moment I understood you and why you did it, but no matter how hard I try it doesn't answer why you stopped loving me, the song leaves me longing fot completion and confused and I finally understood why I'm still madly in love with you.

WORDLESS

I have tried to write a heart breaking poem, where
people feel what I feel. I have tried, but last night as I sat
in front of my type writer, trying to figure out what to
say, I realized I didn't feel anything.
I am hollow.
You took every emotion in me. You took everything and
the only thing remaining is the memories I have of you.
Like the day in the car, where you hand strummed
along to the country song on the radio on my thigh.
Or the time you sang "Whatever it is" to me in my living
room.
You were scared; you feared what we were becoming.
You became too scared to look in my eyes because you
felt something different. Something you can't place, you
still can't.
Was it a friendship or relationship, but now watching
me flirt in the show choir room with people who aren't
you, something about that makes you feel sick.
And that look you give me across the room leaves me
hopeless and confused. How fucking dare you look at me
with those eyes of yours, they once said goodbye and
now they look at me like I am ripping your heart out,
Rewind.
Can we rewind?
Rewind.
Your hand in mine, Lips on my cheek.
Rewind.

"I like you."
Rewind.
"Hey I'm..."
Rewind.
No more pain.
I don't know anymore.

END

Once it's over you think of what you should have said, what you could have said, what you won't get to say.

You get cut off with no real ending.

You shove the blame on each other and go on with your life.

Who knows when it could actually end? Who knows when they will lose what they feel, when someone better comes on through.

Who knows if you've found the one, if it's just a high school lover, or if maybe you will get played? Who knows? It could just end.

When will it end?

EVERY NIGHT I WRITE THIS AND DELETE IT

I FORGOT A LOT OF THINGS IN MY LIFE,
FROM TEST DATES TO BIRTHDAYS, BUT I
CAN'T SEEM TO FORGET THE WAY MY HAND
FELT IN YOURS AND YOU'RE BAD HABIT OF
STAYING UP TOO LATE WATCHING FAST
AND FURIOUS. I LOVED YOU, WITH
EVERYTHING IN ME. I WOULD HAVE GIVEN
YOU THE FUCKING WORLD IF I COULD. BUT
YOU GAVE ONE LOOK AT MY PETHTIC SELF
AND LAUGHED, YOU KNEW WHAT I WAS TO
YOU, AND YET YOU MADE ME BELIEVE I
MEANT SOMETHING, NOW IT'S A YEAR
LATER AND I STILL SMELL YOUR GOD DAMN
SCENT ON MY SHEETS, FEEL YOUR HAND ON
MY THIGH. YOU ARE THE BITTER DARKNESS
THAT CONSUMES ME, I CAN'T EVEN THINK
ABOUT MOVING ON BECAUSE EVERY TIME I
DO, I COMPARE THEM TO YOU. I CAN'T EVEN
WRTE A POEM WITH OUT ME WRITING
ABOUT YOU. YOUR MY BLACK COFFEE, MY
BROKEN RED PEN, RED IS BURNING PASSION
OF LOVE AND THAT'S SOMETHING I
THOUGHT WE FELT BUT I WAS SO TERRIBLY
WRONG. YOU LIED TO ME, YOU LOOKED
INTO MY HAZEL EYES AND LIED. YOU
PROMISED ME FORVER AND NOW I'M
FINDING IT DIFFICULT TO BREATH

BECAUSE YOU WERE MY LUNGS AND YOUR NOT HERE TO SHOW ME HOW TO BREATH. IF I MEANT SOMETHING LIKE YOU SWORE I DID THEN WHY WAS SHE THERE IN THE END. ONE DAY, IT TOOK YOU ONE DAY TO MOVE ON AND IT'S TAKING ME A YEAR. I GAVE YOU PART OF ME, I GAVE YOU A PART OF ME THAT NOBODY COULD EVER FIND EVEN IF THEY DUG THROUGH THE DEEPEST PARTS OF ME, AND YET YOU THREW IT AWAY LIKE THE PIECE OF TRASH IT WAS TO YOU. HOW COULD YOU DO THAT TO ME? HOW COULD YOU WATCH ME CRUMMBLE INTO THE GROUND, I SHOVED EVERYBODY AWAY AFTER YOU AND YET YOU SAT TO THE SIDE, KISSING HER FILTHY MOUTH AND PAID NO ATTENTION TO ME. YOU DON'T CARE AND NEVER DID. AND IF YOU WANT TO KNOW THE HORRIBLE TRUTH OF THE MATTER, I LAUGHED WHEN SHE SCREWED YOU OVER, KARAM RAMMED INTO YOU LIKE YOU RAN INTO ME. I HOPE YOU FEEL HOW I DID, I HOPE YOU CAN SEE WHAT YOU DID TO ME, I HOPE GUILT IS KNOCKING AT YOUR DOOR, AND I SWEAR TO GOD THE DAY YOUAPOLOGIZE TO ME I WILL LAUGH AND NOT RESPOND, HOPEFULLY THAT SMALL AMOUNT OF RESENTMENT WILL PROVE TO YOU HOW MUCH OF A HEARTLESS MONSTER YOU ARE. I FUCKING LOVED YOU. I LOVED YOU. I LOVED YOU WITH EVERY GOD DAMN

PART OF ME AND I HOPE THAT ONE DAY YOU'LL LOOK BACK AT MY MEMORY AND REMEMBER THAT I LOVED YOU. I LOVED YOU AND AS MUCH AS IT BURNS MY SOUL, I STILL DO.

Winter

This morning my mom said it smelt like winter but I inhaled I got the sharp sent of our memories together last snow fall.

I smelt every snowy kiss and snow angel that you messed up by picking me up and whipping away the crystals that started to form on my eyes.

And now here I am, in your sweater from last year's Christmas party, As I sit watching the snow fall. Every snow flake sticking on to me and making an heavy blanket of depression.

I can't help the tears that freeze to my cheeks as if they are clinging on to the last time your hand was there.

Last winter you told me I could tell you anything but how do you expect me to look at you and not crumble because everything I've been feeling is from you.

Every sleepless night, every tear stain pillow case, every hopeless scream that I wish you could hear because I'm drowning in the melted snow of our relationship and I won't be alive to see the spring flowers grow.

Free falling, where is the parachute?

We are speeding down fury ferry, laughing with music blaring; all fun and games until someone gets hurt. Maybe that's my biggest fear, pain. That's why I never attempted to learn how to do a hand stand, in fear I would fall.

I fell.

I fell so hard for you that when I realized I did, my legs wouldn't move to stand me back up. They laid their motionless like the idea of not having you was more terrifying than the idea of being paralyzed.

That's what I am, paralyzed by you. I Thought I could fight but your scent makes my whole world stop. Your laugh ringing in my ears so loudly they bleed.

maybe I'm looking too much into it, I usually am, but I can't help to feel like I've jumped off the cliff and you are the sand at the bottom of my shoes and somewhere inside of me, I'm hoping it will transform into wings so I don't die because I'm facing my biggest fear, falling.

Rescue me please.

I'm scared one day I will have to return your grey t-shirt in a box, along with our two cds and a letter telling you everything that you meant to me.

I'm not scared of the jump I took for you, I'm scared that the ground isn't a pillow of sadness and discomfort and I might actually break a few bones.

The irony in the fact every time I hear tom petty's free falling I think of you and the night we went to the soccer game and yelled the words in my parked car in the school parking lot.

I'm so scared of losing you that I can't even think of
words to explain to you how empty I feel.
And don't think this is my way of telling you I love you,
because those are 3 words I have just learned to mutter
to myself.
I'm saying I have realized that you are the jump I want
to take; I just don't know how far I'm willing to fall.
Sjr / June 22

Broken Hearted

I'm not blaming you, or maybe I am. Before you I could smile, cry and feel alive. But now I stand alone, emotionless, my eyes darker than fresh brewed dark roast. I am nobody now, I'm not saying I'm nobody without you, you took my soul. Left me on the street with nothing but bones, and hollow eyes. My skin still burns from your touch, my life still burning around me. I'm trapped in a room, watching the walls burn down around me, the flames getting close enough to leave my arm hair running but it won't kill me, it won't let me die. It keeps burning me but yet I survive. I survived you. You didn't kill me, you just left me blank. Nothing left, maybe so I can rebuild myself without you, but I can't even find the strength inside me to do that. You left me blank. I know I am supposed to call myself strong for surviving you but I am nothing, nothing but hollow and engulfed in flames, my screams heard everywhere but yet nobody puts them out, nobody can. They wait for me to die, but I can't even mange to do that.

Donald trump.

Today we hear talk about immigration and building walls but what does that really mean?

Maybe immigration is a metaphor for people who can break your heart and walls are our ways of trying to stay safe.

Brick didn't work, maybe i should try concrete

Change

It never occurred to me how much you changed me until I found myself hating peanut butter and jelly sandwiches, because peanut butter and banana is better. I realized you changed me when 26 was my favorite number because that's how many times you read each book you owned. I never realized I was someone new until I let myself cry at dead flowers and I couldn't fall asleep without watching Scooby Doo reruns. Rainy days became my favorite because they reminded you that the world is capable of tears. Blue is my favorite color because it was yours. And I now agree, vinyl is so much better than cd's. Tumblr is not a social media to me; it's a way of life. And I don't ever leave the house without my lucky penny. I have a jar, just like you did, that collects money on my shelf for the adventure we always planned and god dammit I bought Christmas lights for my room because yours was covered head to toe. I don't drink soda out of a can unless it has a straw and I think spoons are cooler than forks. Gucci became a constant vocabulary and I always bit my lip when thinking. It's almost as since you left, I can't cope with not having you so I am becoming you.

Forgetting the unforgotten

I spent all my time hating her for taking you from me.
I loathed her.
But I realized she isn't why I'm upset.
It's you.
You left me stranded with nothing but memories and a guitar pick.
I placed the guitar pick on my car keys so I could be reminded of you every time I tried to leave this town.
You're holding me back but I was too blinded by fake hatred and fantasy.
If you truly loved me than you wouldn't be with her.
She didn't make you do anything; you left on your own.
So I don't know why I looked at that smile you have when you see her and think
"She's tricking him."
When in Realty I used her to cover of up the truth of it.
I didn't want to realize you left me because I wasn't good enough.
You left me.
And because of that, I'm a shadow in the darkness; an empty void consumes me because I am an idiot.
With a problem of covering up all the wrong I do with theories that never make sense, except in my mind.
That is trying so hard to get my heart to work again but little does it know, it's crushing it by not being able to forget & making up lies that I'll soon find out fake and have to be faced with the long, never ending pain of once loving you

GREY

You left me with scratchy memories and an old torn t-shirt.
The scent of your polo cologne still sticking to the grey fabric as if it was holding on for dear life. Just like me, but instead of life I cling on to that grey old t-shirt taking in whiffs of what use to be.
The memories bleed through the fabric and onto me ending as salty tears.
It stays crumbled in the corner, calling for me and leaving the scratchy memories of loving you.
As I run the weak fabric through my hands images of you appear leaving me crumbled just like the old t-shirt and leaving my mind wonder, facing 'what if's in the black heart that matches the black stain on the collar.
I wear it to bed just so maybe it will feel the same as when I wore it when I had you.
I know I am bullshitting myself once again and it's going to leave me with red eyes and a wet pillow case all because I can't let go of this stupid grey t-shirt that has taken over me because you walked out on me and left me with a dumb old t-shirt that smells of polo cologne and tears with the faint hint feeling of happiness because of the scratchy memories that remain within but I'll never rid myself of black stained, torn, polo scented old grey t-shirt because it leaves me with the ever so faint memories of loving you.

Reawakened

Someone opened a window
And cleared the suffocating smoke that lingered after your memories
I've taken the first sip of water and I crave redemption
and I'm ready to move on from you and your demons.

Refrigerator love

When my days are cold and I'm alone, your thoughts seem to enter me and leave me puzzled but I am determined to solve you like my mother solves the Sunday paper's crossword puzzle. And when I solve you I will hang you on the fridge next to my sister's art work so everyone can admire you.

Blind

You said I was blind to feelings, but I got glasses and I can now see you never loved me.

How am I supposed to cope with loosing something that was never mine?

How do you wake up in the morning and tell yourself you shouldn't be feeling this much pain, as if lying to yourself can make all your problems go away.
I have gotten good at that, telling myself that I'm not drowning form the inside out but lack of sleep coming to claim my lifeless soul.

And you would think that out of all the tears I've shed, the fire on my skin from your touch would hsve died out but it's been 3 damn months and I still feel the painting on my back your fingertips carved there. You would think that it would have died out from the coldness of my soul but the last remaining love I have for you is fueling this wild fire of self-hatred for me being dumb enough to trust you with a box of matches and my heart.

I will.

Some nights I will stay up late because my skin is
burning from where you once kissed it.
My collar bones hurt the worse.
I will shiver from the still haunting feeling of your
fingertips gliding up my leg. Almost like little shocks of
electricity.
I will scream because I still feel the agenizing pain from
when you lite my heart on fire. Instead of blowing it out,
you let it keep burning, until the small flame took over
my body and burned my soul a terrifying black.
I will cry until the sun is coming back up because I can
no longer find myself, lost in promise un-kept and
unending hopelessness, leaving me robotically hollow.
And I will hug myself because my crushed pieces no
longer are held together by you.
I will stare at my phone until my eyes ache from not
blinking because you haven't texted me at all.
I will whisper your name or bring it up in random
conversation because I miss saying it.
Oh how I miss you,
You
You.

Untitled: just like us.

You were gone as soon as you came
Like a breeze upon a hot summers day.
And I've gotten better at ignoring the memories that
flow through my hair, as I sit drinking my lemonade.
Your favorite, the irony.

You keep knocking on the door to my heart,
Begging for the key to unlock it.
I locked you out the last time you left.
Knock knock knock
You never stop trying.
"Why have you given up on me?" you scream.
But did you ever stop and think that maybe you've given
up on me?

After all the time you've lite me on fire to keep you
warm from your freezing heart, I still stood back up
afterwards and kissed your cheek.
But that final time you kept laughing as I yelled out in
heart breaking pain, I knew I was finally done with your
arduous heart breaking game.

Map less.

I will get in my car at 2 am

And drive with the headlights off

Until I reach the end.

The only thing keeping me going is a half tank of gas and an guitar pick you gave me when we were just friends.

My hands are shaky and my stomach is aching from sobs.

Its 2am and I am almost gone

Because you're the highway and I'm the idiotic one driving with no headlights and the two things that keep me going is an half empty tank of love and an old guitar pick.

Wonder.

I wonder if you got your tattoo removed, the one that
matched the black ink stained on my wrist.
My constant reminder of not being good enough.

"We're just not a perfect fit."

But truth be told, we were. Before your drunken words
bent me with every punch, every harsh word.

I wonder if my initial is still hanging from your car keys
or did you throw it out long ago?
Did it remind you of me? McDonald's runs and Céline
Dion repeats.

All the wonders I have for you and I guess, I suppose,
that I'm still in love with you even though you broke
me.

Sleep.

I've been sleep walking in the memory of you.
I am stumbling on the hard wood floors to the liquor cabinet of time. As if a shot of whiskey could match the burning I once felt in the pit of my stomach when I saw your hazel eyes looking into mine.

"I need to see you one last time as mine." I say trying to convince myself I won't dream of you tomorrow night, or the next and the next, that this is the last time.

I know it only causes the numbness in my body to grow more numb. It only causes my tears to freeze at how cold you once were to me. But I rather freeze in your memory than be sweating in the heat of losing you.

I need to feel you, see you the look you once gave me when my dreams were reality. When slow dancing came naturally and I wasn't choking on the words "I think you are my soul mate."

When calling at 3am because my voice helped you sleep wasn't a dial tone of words I could never say to you.

I need to talk to you, the way I use to. Watch your brows merge together as you thought carefully of what to say back to me because you know words are sharp knives pressed to my neck.

I need to see the right part of your mouth quirk up across a room full of people that I didn't notice were there until I realized that I was running in place towards you and they won't let go of my arms.

I need to connect my eyes to your eyes, specks of gold reaching into me as if I was standing close enough to a wild fire to breath in the heat, singe my arm hairs, but never fully burn me. You wouldn't let me go that way.

No, you had to make sure I lived my life underwater, gasping for air, pulling me out just before I drowned just so you could feel the connection as you distilled all meaning from inside of me.

I stumble on the hard wood floors; my socks making me slip as I am reaching for the handle of the door.

And when I finally mange to lift myself and open the door in hopes you haven't left yet, I see the dust still dancing in the air from the spinning of the tires as you drive away in your car named trust, on a road named us, heading to the destination of forgetting the one you said you loved.

Reason why 'Lilac Skies':

I have a obsession with sunsets and sunrises, mainly sunsets. I have over 500 pictures of sunsets alone on my phone and have gone "sunset chasing" before.

Lilac Skies comes from memory of someone asking me what sunset was my favorite and I said "Lilac skies". Something about the color always puts me at peace enough to reflect on my past. It represents love to me and so much more.

It's who I am.

x. sarah

Acknowledgements:

I want to share my thanks to the following:

My loving family: Thank you for constantly pushing me to take grasp of my dreams and making sure I didn't fall back but only kept moving forward. I love each and every one of you "fooks".

Katie: Thank you for sticking by my side for 10 years, your friendship is truly a blessing. Thank you for being my sister and best friend but also teaching me to let go and move on from things in the past. You are so strong and it truly impacts everyone you meet.

Anna: Thank you for the support you have shown me in all my life decisions and have had my back for the years we have been friends. Thank you for accepting my random "gossip girl" texts and always being down for jam sessions, poetry rants and random kidnaps. Thank you for countless date nights and being my shoulder to cry on. I love you.

Price: Thank you for being my best friend and loving my crazy self. Thank you for our inside puns and never leaving me stranded. You make afternoon car rides fun and honestly are such a blessing to my life. You have been there for me in my lowest point and I will always love you for that.

To my group chat (You girls know who you are): Thank you for being a HUGE support group. The amount of love and care for each other in the chat is beyond beautiful. Thank you for always being there and giving me a laugh when it was deathly needed. Thank you for teaching me to love myself and looking at myself as the "Prada" person I am. You all are sweet, beautiful and loving. I hope you all continue to be so. Love you all so dearly and thank you for all you girls have done.

William: Thank you. Thank you for believing in me and showing me an enormous amount of love. You truly are such an amazing person who has so much in store for them. Thank you for being my shoulder to cry on, my support system, my boyfriend at one point, and my best friend. Thank you for your phone conversations and endless hours of hanging out. Thank you for inside jokes, Mexican & Jason Deli dates. Thank you for coming into my life and not changing me but loving me for me. Thank you William Billue for being you.

Last but not least, Mr. Davis: Thank you for being always a farther figure and helping me to fall more in love with the art of writing. Thank you for always encouraging me and nagging me about my spelling. Thank you for not only being a role model students and I look up to, but treating students with respect. Thank you for finding the talent in each and every student and for making sure they show their full potential. You future students will be so lucky to have you as a teacher.

Thank you to everyone not included in this list. You all have impacted my life in some shape or form. Everything each person has brought me has taught me so much.

I love all of you deeply and thank you for riding this journey with me.

x. Sarah

About the Author:

Sarah Reese was born in Summerville South Carolina on August 18th 1998 and lived there until she was one, she then moved to Greenville South Carolina where she spent most of her childhood. When she turned 14, she moved to Augusta Georgia where she now lives. Sarah is the daughter of Chuck and Stephanie Reese. She is the baby of the family with 3 older half-sisters and a brother. Sarah enjoys her time writing poetry, hanging out with her friends and watching UGA college football.

Sarah wants to attend college at Georgia Southern University for two years before transferring to University of Georgia to major in Journalism and minor in English.

"I come from a family of educators so I think they all want me teaching one day but in my own dreams I hope to be reporting on world news one day, be able to travel the words and write. That would be my dream comes true."

Sarah has been involved in writing since you was little and was even manager of the Hillcrest High School Speech and Debate team in only 7th grade.

When asked what helped her most to write she said "Classical music for sure, it helps me keep focus, Also just my emotions. A lot of what I write about is how I feel, maybe a tad bit over the top how I feel but defiantly how I feel. "